To Bets,
Hope this brings
back pleasant
memories

love Trish

It's Magic

Cinderella, King Arthur, and the Seven Dwarfs would all feel at home in this fantasy land of nature and legend. Here wind and wave, rain and river have sculptured a tropical island into the kind of faerie-like reality that magic is made of. The romantic appeal of Kauai's tawny beaches, the spectacular grandeur of Waimea Canyon, and the poetry of the mist-shrouded Napali Cliffs have excited the human imagination since Hawaiians first waded ashore more than 1,500 years ago.

Now it's your turn. This book is your personal guide to the special magic we call Kauai.

KAUAI

Text / BOB KRAUSS
Photography / BILL GLEASNER

AN
ISLAND
HERITAGE BOOK

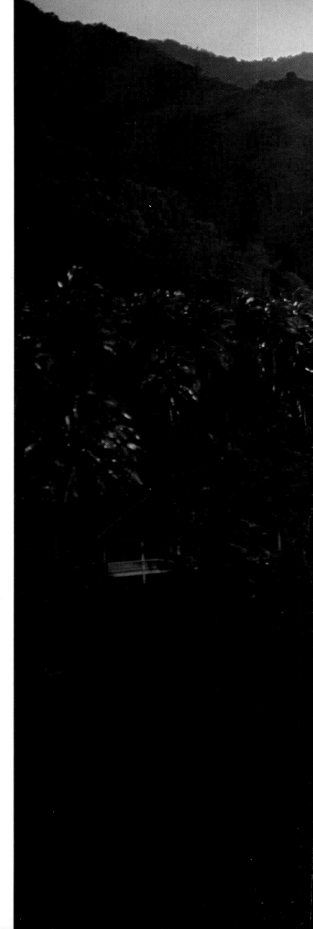

*RAIN-LACED SEA BREEZES rustle the
sheltering palm trees of an island homesite.*

Acknowledgements:

Island Heritage would like
to thank June Gutmanis
for her research into
Hawaiian chants on Kauai,
and Gordon Ng of Color
Prints for his help on the
reproductions in this book.
In addition, we would like
to thank all those on
Kauai who helped
introduce us to the many
charms of this special
Hawaiian island.

Produced and published by
Island Heritage Limited
Robert B. Goodman and
Robert A. Spicer, Publishers

Norfolk Island Office
'Leeside' Taylors Road
Norfolk Island 2899
Australia

Please address orders and editorial
correspondence to our United States office:
Island Heritage Limited
324 Kamani Street
Honolulu, Hawaii 96813
Phone: (808) 533-4211
Cable: HAWAIIBOOK
Telex: Heritage 634206

Trade Ed: ISBN 0-89610-067-7
Special Ed: ISBN 0-89610-070-7
Japanese Ed: ISBN 0-89610-071-5

CONTENTS

THE STORY OF AN ISLAND

YOUR GUIDE TO KAUAI

6

A GARLAND OF MIST drapes the cliffs of Kauai's Napali Coast. Overleaf, a quiet valley, edged by a summer sea, catches the last moment of the evening sun.

Bali Hai

K auai is the Bali Hai picture postcard image of the South Seas. The love story *South Pacific* was filmed here, for of all the Hawaiian islands, Kauai comes closest to being everyone's dream of a tropical paradise. Here, the living is easy and overcoats are excess baggage. The lushness of Kauai's foliage and an abundance of flowers long ago earned its reputation as "The Garden Island."

The story of Kauai began more than 10 million years ago when, in the black depths of the Pacific, a volcano ripped open the ocean floor. For about two million years the monster spewed out molten lava, building an enormous undersea mountain. When the tip broke out, hissing and steaming in the brilliant sunlight, beneath it lay an underwater mountain that had risen nearly 3 miles from the bottom of the sea.

The eruptions continued. For eight million more years lava piled up until, high above the ocean, a new island was born.

This barren, near circular volcano, first of those islands to be called Hawaiian, was now exposed to the forces that were to give it character and beauty. The great dome of raw lava was thrust up directly into the path of the prevailing trade winds. These moisture-laden winds, a never failing sun, and giant waves generated by 2,000 miles of fetch, were now ready to work their magic.

HER CALDERA FILLED with cloud (above), Mount Waialeale stands in lonely grandeur. At right, rainwater, like rivulets of molten silver, scores Waialeale's vertical face.

A rugged remnant of the volcano that formed Kauai is a 5,150-foot mountain which dominates the island's landscape. It has been named Mount Waialeale (meaning rippling waters). Because the mountaintop was constantly shrouded in clouds, the ancient Hawaiians believed that the gods met there to plot the fate of the island. Whether from the gods or the heavy cloud formations, Waialeale is one of the wettest spots on earth. About 460 inches of rain fall there every year. And every year for several million years, that rain has coursed down the sides of the mountain—carving, gouging, scraping, eroding the wild and beautiful canyons that characterize Kauai.

The crater atop the mountain which once belched fire and lava is now an eerie marsh—a 30 square mile area called Alakai Swamp. Heavy rains have long since quenched the volcanic fires and the present day bog could easily be the Sherlock Holmes setting for the *Hound of the Baskervilles.* It is a place of rain and mist and mud and fern and moss. Plant forms are grotesque. Mature trees grow only knee high. There are no landmarks. Only the most experienced may trek across this trackless, treacherous wasteland.

Like so many spokes of a wagon wheel, seven rivers fan out from the Alakai Swamp to return the rainwater to the sea. First as tiny, sparkling rivulets, they quietly slip out of the swamp; then, responding to the force of gravity, they start their wild, turbulent plunge down the precipitous sides of the mountain.

The spectacular waterfalls and color-splashed canyons that have been carved out of this ancient volcanic mountain are world famous. And far below, mud and silt, twigs and tiny particles of decomposed lava—debris from this mighty sculptor's work—have spread out to make the broad fertile fields of The Garden Isle.

While the rippling waters of Waialeale were at work sculpturing the island, the

northeast trade winds were also busy. Year after year, wind driven waves ate away at the north edge of the island until it became a steep embankment. Then the waves dug away the embankment until it collapsed into the sea. The battering assault by the sea continued for ages. Finally, only stark, vertical cliffs remained. These huge black buttresses give their name to 15 miles of spectacular wilderness called the Napali (the cliff) Coast.

A RELENTLESS RUSH OF WATER (left) laden with silt plunges toward the sea. Below: Softened by the touch of a rainbow, stand the razored ridges of the Napali Coast.

In silent majesty the cliffs rise to 3,000 feet, like sentinels standing guard at the mouths of soaring valleys of Mount Waialeale.

The process goes on.

Waves still explode at the base of the cliffs while, deep in the valleys, waterfalls eat relentlessly into the high uplands. Fortunately for all of us, this terrain is so rugged that freeways and suburbs have never penetrated here. Its natural beauty beckons to visitor and resident alike, but you can enter the Napali Coast only by boat, on foot, by helicopter or in your imagination from a viewpoint high above Kalalau Valley.

*WINTER STORM WAVES THUNDER
against Napali's buttressed cliffs. Below:
Its fury spent, a winter wave surges back
to the sea.*

WAIMEA CANYON LAYS BARE the layers of Kauai's volcanic history. Nearly 3,000 feet deep, and colored in shades of ochre, rust and brown, the canyon snakes 14 miles across Kauai's western end.

*LACY WATERS of Hanakapiai
Falls cascade toward the sea.
At right, the Kauai 'O'O,*
Moho braccatus, *is
found today only
in the forests of the
Alakai Swamp.
Below, the 'Akialoa,*
Hemignathus procerus,
*is very rare and
known to live only
in the upper rain
forests of Kauai. It
was last seen in 1960.*

A side from the tiny creatures that crawled up from the sea, the first arrivals to this new land came probably by chance—migrating birds blown off course; pelagic birds tirelessly sweeping the ocean in search of food; or hapless flocks of land birds caught in freakish winds.

Today, Kauai is a veritable aviary, ranging from nesting sea birds, migrating ducks, wintering plovers, marvelously endowed indigenous birds that have evolved here, to the wide variety of exotic birds introduced since man first came ashore.

Perhaps unequaled in the world, Kauai's colorful bird population will delight you with song, plumage and form.

When, how, in what form, plant life first appeared on this lonely, barren volcanic island is open to speculation. However, growing conditions were ideal.

19

EARLY POLYNESIAN VOYAGERS,
probably from the Marquesas, unload
their precious cargo of food plants. At
right: Taro, the plant from which poi is
made, grows in foot-deep water. At far
right, a stalk of ripening banana.

It is likely that the early bird visitors brought more than song and feather. While the question is still open to speculation, birds probably were bearers of the seed and spore that gave rise to some of the first plant life here. After all, growing conditions on this lonely, barren, volcanic island were ideal. And the process gained momentum when the old Hawaiians brought with them seeds and plants needed for survival.

They brought the proud, waist high taro plant that produces a nourishing tuber underground. The coconut palm, tall and graceful, produced nourishing drink, meat to eat,

Painting by Herb Kawainui Kane.

leaves for thatching, nuts for use as dishes, and wood used in carpentry. A giant grass called sugar cane provided windbreaks for taro patches and sweet fiber to chew. The stately canopy of the breadfruit tree made shade and gave nutritious food as well. Giant

banana leaves were used in underground ovens. The bananas were eaten raw or cooked. Sweet potato vines hugged the ground, drawing moisture that produced food without irrigation. The stalks of ti plants, their baked roots an insurance against famine, grew everywhere in sturdy defiance of evil spirits. All these new plants flourished on the island and added texture to Kauai's wardrobe.

The old Hawaiians brought few flowers. So utilitarian plants had to do double duty. The hala tree yielded not only tough leaves for weaving mats and sails but decorative orange seeds used for personal adornment. Hawaiians exploited the beauty of tiny wild flowers and native ferns, even leaves and twigs, in making garlands to wear on their heads and wrists and around their necks.

Left (from top, counterclockwise), Kou, Noni, Ukiuiki, and at right, Pandanus tree, also known as Hala.

But it remained for the white men, who followed the path of Captain James Cook in 1778, to bring exotic flowers to Kauai. These blossoms were welcomed with enthusiasm by Hawaiians. Kauai's roadsides and gardens are ablaze today with the colors of flowering trees and shrubs and vines from around the world.

June is the most spectacular month for blossoms on Kauai. This is the time that the royal poinciana (Madagascar), pink and white shower trees (Java and Sumatra), the golden shower (India), pink Bauhinia (Central America), and oleander (Iran) are at the peak of their blooming. In January the orange trumpet vine (Brazil) blooms on the stone wall along the Poipu Road. Spring brings to life the tabebuia or gold trees (Mexico) in Waimea and Lihue. Kauai natives can also tell you that the bougainvillea (Brazil) in Waimea blooms in March, the royal poinciana (Madagascar) in the Lihue Union Church grounds in June, night-blooming cereus (Mexico) on Grove Farm Road during August, rainbow shower trees (hybrid) on the Waimea School campus in late summer, and the foamy white porana vine (India) on Grove Farm Road in late October. Of course, the hibiscus and plumeria and orchids bloom almost all year long. Each adds its splash of color to the tropical jungle that has embraced the bare lava of that long ago volcano.

As you can see, the magic of Kauai is made up of many ingredients: awesome valleys, looming cliffs, tropical foliage, musical bird-songs, silvery waterfalls, exotic blossoms. But the most essential ingredient is you yourself.

TORCH GINGER, Cup of Gold, and Red Jade Vine bloom in the Olo Pua Garden.

*THE APPROACHING NIGHT gilds a
rock pinnacle with the last rays of
the sun. Right, secret Kauai beaches
are colored by a mist-softened sunset.*

Kalalau Valley is just the name of a place
on a map until you stand in the bracing air of
the lookout above and let your eye follow the
breathtaking curve of a mountain ridge to
the edge of the cliff. There is really no way to
experience Napali Coast until you stand in
its lonely presence and feel the shock of a
wave exploding against a cliff. The full
dimension of Kauai's magic comes alive only
in the personal experience, the imagination,
the humor and the spiritual sensitivity of
people who come here.

It has been so since the time of the ancient
Hawaiians. For them, the valleys had
power of speech, the cliffs were alive with
spirits, and rocks might jump up and do
tricks. The Hawaiians lavished on Kauai an
imaginative literature of legend that is bigger
than human, often humorous and always
rooted in the truth.

It is no coincidence that Haena, a coastline
of palm shaded beaches where the Bali Hai
scene in *South Pacific* was filmed, was also
the stage for Kauai's Hawaiian heroes and
heroines. Haena was the place where Pele,
the great goddess of volcanoes, came to find
a home in the Hawaiian Islands.

Pele first dug a cave back of the beach,
hoping to set up housekeeping. But she struck
water. She dug another cave nearby with the
same result. Disgusted, she abandoned Kauai
and travelled south from one island to
another until she found a suitable dwelling in
the firepit of Halemaumau on the island of
Hawaii. Her abandoned homes, the Wet
Caves at Haena, are still there.

The sensual throb of the surf on Haena
Beach continued to arouse romantic thoughts
about the puckish Pele. One day Pele returned
to this spot as a wandering spirit at a time
when a great ceremony was in progress. As
she watched the festivities, Pele was capti-
vated by Lohiau, the handsome young Hawaiian chief in charge of the ceremony. The
passionate goddess just had to have him, but
she could not enjoy him while in spirit form.
So she hurried back to her firepit and sent
her sister, Hiiaka, to bring Lohiau back. The
plot thickened when Hiiaka fell in love with
Lohiau. Pele suspected as much. In revenge,
she made Halemaumau erupt. The climax
came when Hiiaka returned with Lohiau and,
in the midst of the volcano eruption, made
love to him on the edge of the firepit.

This legend will give you some idea of the
zest and enthusiasm with which the Hawaiians have responded to the romantic beaches
of Haena.

Many of Kauai's legends have a tongue-in-cheek quality that turns magic into a smile. The shelf of black rock on Lumahai Beach is all that is left of a disreputable giant with a very foul mouth. He was forever sticking his tongue out at people and calling them names. Finally, another giant dispatched the obnoxious fellow and threw his body to the sharks. They ate all of him but his tongue which they found too bitter. It is there to this day.

The Spouting Horn, a regular stop for tour buses, is a lava tube on the Koloa Shore where waves enter an underwater cave and force plumes of spray up through the hole. Air sucked through the hole produces a doleful, moaning sound. The old Hawaiians invented a more colorful explanation. In the legend, the moaning is that of a soft-hearted mo'o (large supernatural lizard) who became distraught by the death of two sister mo'os on nearby Niihau.

The tendency on Kauai to deal with magic on a first name basis still abounds. A good example is the torchlighting ceremony. This is a Kauai tradition that started only 25 years ago when an energetic woman with the soul of a Hawaiian priestess took over a seedy bar and restaurant near the mouth of the Wailua River. Her name is Grace Buscher Guslander. She converted the cafe into a hotel called Coco Palms, turned the canal into a romantic lagoon and the plantation into shady coconut grove. Still, she wasn't satisfied. A special Hawaiian touch was needed.

One evening before dinner she dressed up two busboys and the bartender in malos (breechclouts). At sundown, she had the busboys run along the banks of the lagoon lighting torches while the bartender blew a conch shell. The diners were spellbound. It would have been impossible to convince any of them that this was not an ancient rite handed down through the generations.

Today, this "authentic" torchlighting ceremony has become a Coco Palms tradition copied by hotels all over the state, an example of Kauai magic in action.

BIRD'S-EYE VIEW (left) looking west from Hanalei Bay toward Haena. Above, The Spouting Horn.

BOULDER-STREWN STREAM BED in forest of Hanakapiai Valley. Below, Alekoko Fishpond. Hand built wall is in picture's left center.

Menehune

Picture a fellow two or three feet tall, stout, potbellied, muscular, with a hairy body and large eyes hidden by bushy eyebrows in a red face, with a short, thick nose. Such is the description given by J.H. Kaiwi whose grandparents said they met some Menehunes while gathering sandalwood in the mountain forests of Kauai. Of all the Kauai characters who have captured the imagination, the Menehunes are the most famous.

Menehunes have been reported on all of the islands in Hawaii but Kauai is their favorite. Many legendary feats have been attributed to them. They are very shy, work only at night, and hide in the forest during the day. Their excellence as stone masons is seen in the impressive Menehune Ditch. This structure is an aqueduct constructed in Waimea Valley during legendary times under the reign of a high chief named Ola. In 1793

Captain George Vancouver, the British explorer, described this irrigation ditch as "an exceedingly well constructed wall of stones and clay about 24 feet high, raised from the bottom by the side of the cliff (and) served not only as a pass into the country (valley) but also as an aqueduct to convey the water thither by great labor (sic) from a considerable distance." Today only a few stones are still in place. They are cut and fitted with a skill the Hawaiians have forgotten or never knew.

Who built this wall?

The popular theory is that an early race of small, inferior Polynesians built the wall. This theory is supported by the fact that the lowest class of society in Tahiti were called "manahune." Commoners in Polynesia were traditionally of smaller stature than the better fed chiefs.

Suppose the first settlers in Hawaii were commoners who excelled in stone work. Suppose further that later arrivals who were larger and stronger drove the first arrivals from their homes and into the mountains where they hid in the forest. Suppose also that these inferior people were put to work building irrigation ditches and temples. In time the race died out or merged with the late arrivals. But they survived in legend, even smaller than they had been in real life and invested with superhuman strength.

Another famous Menehune project is the Alekoko Fish Pond up river from Nawiliwili Harbor. The fish pond, an example of early aquaculture, was made by cutting off a bend in the river with a wall more than 900 feet long. The wall is built of dirt faced with stone to a height of five feet above water level and four feet wide on top. According to the legend, the stones for the wall came from Makaweli, 25 miles distant, and were passed from hand to hand along a double row of Menehune workmen.

How much of this is fact and how much fiction? Two Polynesian authorities offer opposing arguments. Katharine Luomala points out that archaeology in the Hawaiian Islands has never unearthed skeletons of a race of people two or three feet tall. Also, the manahunes of Tahiti were not skilled stone workers. Her conclusion is, "There is nothing to prove that they (Menehunes) were ever real people. They are the products of human imagination, and considering the lack of any good evidence to the contrary, the only conclusion possible is that they are mythical people invented by storytellers."

On the other hand, the famed Polynesian anthropologist Peter Buck argued convincingly that, "The Menehune were real, live people of Polynesian stock, and they are entitled to the honour and glory of being the first to cross the ocean wastes to Hawaii."

Paintings, pp. 34, 36-37, 38, by Herb Kawainui Kane.

The First Hawaiians

The unwritten but not unrecorded history of man in Hawaii pre-dates by more than a thousand years the arrival of Captain Cook in 1778. The pre-contact period, largely recorded in chant, ritual and artifact, is in many ways more interesting than what has happened since. The contrast between the old culture and the "civilization" that followed is indeed dramatic.

The old culture began about 500 A.D. when the first settlers, probably from the Marquesas Islands, landed in double-hulled outrigger canoes after a voyage of over 2,000 miles. Another wave of immigrants came about 1200 A.D. from Tahiti.

The early inhabitants were isolated from the rest of the world. Their situation was similar to that of modern earthlings trying to survive on a tiny planet spinning alone in space. The natural resources of the island were limited. If resources ran out, they could not be replaced.

The ancient Hawaiian showed a great deal of skill in adapting to the limitations. Since he had no iron, he used stone, bone and wood. Archaeological digs on the Napali Coast have yielded beautifully carved fishhooks, stone tools, files made of coral and sea urchin spines, coral sanders and hand drills with bone and stone bits. You can see some of these implements at the Kauai Museum in Lihue.

By the time the white man arrived, the Hawaiian on Kauai had inhabited every corner of the island. The Napali Coast, uninhabited today except for campers, supported a sizable population of Hawaiians. Kalalau Valley was extensively terraced and irrigated. Another valley down the coast, Nualolo Kai, was so cut off by steep cliffs that inhabitants had to come in on a rope ladder. Yet, the valley is terraced for growing taro. On Kauai, some Hawaiians even settled far inland, away from the sea. This did not happen on the other islands.

These people raised taro, sugar cane and bananas. The sweet potato, never irrigated, was the poor man's crop. Besides fish, the only meats available to the early inhabitants were pig, dog and chicken. All the evidence indicates that the old Hawaiian was a superb gardener. He knew 300 varieties of taro. He developed sophisticated irrigation systems, but most of these are overgrown today. The view from a lookout above Hanalei Valley still gives an impression of what an agricultural complex must have looked like 500 years ago. Below you, the river winds peacefully among taro patches irrigated by an intricate series of ditches. Blue-green mountains, laced with waterfalls in the rainy season, rise from the floor of the valley. The scene is one of contentment and tranquility.

Hanalei Valley is also a good place to learn

about the economic system evolved by the old Hawaiian. Self-sufficiency was essential. To accomplish this, a system of land use evolved that was very different from today. Hanalei Valley is an ecosystem that reaches from the beach to the mountains. Here the inhabitants could catch fish, grow food crops and livestock, hew canoe logs and house posts in the mountains and in general meet all their needs for survival. Such land units were called ahupua'as. The entire island was divided into such self-sufficient parcels, each producing all the resources the island had to offer.

The residents of such parcels, the ohana, were an extended family joined by the common need to survive. Within the ohana, the technique of exchange in value was gift-giving. A fisherman shared his catch with a relative or friend who grew taro up the valley. A farmer took several bundles of taro as gifts when he went visiting on the beach. The giving of a gift was like a deposit in the bank. It would come back with interest. A selfish person without friends was the one who did not survive in times of famine. This technique of economic survival is best expressed in a

philosophy common among Polynesians throughout the Pacific, "We feast or starve together."

Kauai's remoteness put a special stamp on its people. On all the islands, chiefs were descended from the gods. But the chiefs of Kauai were the most sacred of all because their blood lines were the purest. They were eagerly sought as marriage partners by chiefly social climbers on other islands. Also, Kauai was never invaded successfully, which further enhanced the prestige of Kauai. Her chiefs remained traditionally independent, a breed apart; the purest of the blue blood of Hawaiian aristocracy.

Such were the kind of people who greeted Cook with astonishment when he anchored in Waimea Bay.

THE ANCESTRAL POLYNESIAN developed a highly sophisticated culture filled with science, ritual, storytelling, and dance.

A New Society

F ew of the white men who followed Cook understood the impact they were making upon these newly discovered islands. The potential for profits brought trading ships from many nations into the Pacific. Waimea, Kauai became a popular port of call on voyages between the Northwest and Canton, China, because of the abundance of fresh provisions for sale, the eager hospitality of the women and the friendliness of the ruling chief, Kaeo.

Starting in 1786 the Hawaiians on Kauai eagerly traded hogs, sweet potatoes, taro and handwoven cordage (useful for rigging) for bits of iron which they turned into fishhooks and cutting tools. Inflation set in when Chief Kaeo learned how desperately the ship cap-

tains needed fresh provisions. By 1789 he was demanding and getting an iron bar 18 inches long for a medium-sized hog.

In 1791 one of the captains discovered sticks of sandalwood in a load of firewood he had purchased on Kauai. Soon ship captains began negotiating with chiefs for sandalwood which brought a good price in Canton.

The Hawaiian chiefs were given fancy uniforms, ornate furniture, bolts of bright colored cloth and other gaudy trinkets in addition to liquor. The greediness with which the chiefs sought this new wealth became a curse to the common Hawaiians who were forced to neglect their taro patches while cutting sandalwood high up in the wet, cold mountains. This new hardship, together with

39

the white man's lethal diseases, contributed to a drastic population decrease.

Very quickly, guns became the trade goods most eagerly sought by the chiefs. In the 1790's, firearms were demanded for hogs while iron brought vegetables. The use of firearms obviously increased the number of warriors killed in battles which had formerly been fought with spears and clubs and sling stones. Because Hawaiian warriors were not skilled with guns, the local chiefs hired sailors to fight as mercenaries. Most of these men were mutineers or misfits whose undisciplined conduct added new vices to those the Hawaiians knew already.

The first serious threat to Kauai's sovereignty came from the mighty Kamehameha. After conquering Maui and Oahu, he looked to Kauai. His invasion fleet set sail from Waianae, Oahu, in April, 1796. A storm

KAMEHAMEHA
An original painting by Joseph Feher.

wrecked Kamehameha's plan and his canoes. So he assembled another fleet. This time 800 canoes, especially designed for rough water, set out in 1804. Again fate intervened. His army was decimated by an epidemic, probably cholera. Undaunted by repeated failure, Kamehameha began to put together an armada of sailing vessels built at Waikiki by foreigners in his service.

By this time, Kaumualii, the chief of Kauai, could see the handwriting on the wall. To avoid being conquered, he signed a treaty with Kamehameha under which Kaumualii remained as head man on Kauai but pledged allegiance to the Hawaii chief.

A new political element was added when a Russian agent, George Anton Scheffer, arrived on Kauai with orders to establish a foothold. He worked himself into the good graces of Kaumualii, and then built a large fort on a bluff overlooking Waimea Bay where the guns could command the anchorage for trading vessels. Scheffer promised Kaumualii independence from Kamehameha in return for a trade monopoly with the Russians. Apparently, Kaumualii agreed. For about a year Scheffer was virtual ruler of Kauai. Eventually, Kaumualii regretted the agreement and sent Scheffer packing. The ruins of the Russian fort remain as a relic of the first attempt at foreign meddling in Hawaiian affairs.

Kamehameha died in 1819. His son, Liholiho, became the ruler of Hawaii. Liholiho did not trust Kaumualii so he lured the Kauai chief aboard the royal yacht and took him to Oahu as a prisoner, where he died three years later. Kaumualii's son, Humehume, made a final bid for independence in 1824. His revolt was crushed and Humehume was captured. Kauai finally became part of the larger world.

In 1820 the first missionaries arrived on the island. They set up a station at Waimea. A trade school followed at Hanalei in 1834 and a boarding school at Koloa in 1835. By midcentury, Kauai was almost as literate a place as New England.

But the remote little island was still an economic backwater. The sandalwood trees had all been cut. Whaling provided very little stimulus. A steady stream of optimists tried raising various crops but found great difficulty getting the crops to market. In 1835 plantation owners built a primitive sugar mill at Koloa. The old mill still stands in the center of the village.

The first real success at growing sugar cane as a commercial crop came in the 1850's at Lihue Plantation where a former missionary, William Harrison Rice, dug the first irrigation ditch to water the cane. Cane requires two years to ripen and needs regular irrigation. By tapping the abundant stream water on Kauai, Rice made his crop immune to drought and so the plantation prospered.

Young George Wilcox, who bought Grove

Farm in the 1860's, imitated Rice's irrigation methods. He, too, prospered. Yet, the operation was primitive. Ox carts used to haul sugar cane moved at one mile an hour, which meant that fields had to be very close to the mill. The speed of an ox cart severely limited the size of the plantations.

Today Grove Farm Homestead, on the outskirts of Lihue, is being turned into a museum depicting the history of the sugar industry on Kauai.

VILLAGE OF WAIMEA, KAUAI, in mid-1800's. Note Russian Fort at far left, flag flying. Below, American Mission Church, 1850.

The sugar story is a colorful one. Steam plows replaced oxen. Tiny locomotives replaced ox carts and permitted an expansion of acreage. The impetus given by steam locomotives was strengthened by the price of sugar. For years, sugar planters in Hawaii sought favorable treatment in the U.S. market. Finally, in 1876, King Kalakaua negotiated a treaty permitting Hawaiian sugar to enter the U.S. duty free in return for the use of Pearl Harbor as a naval base. Profits soared. It was on this economic vigor that Kauai rode into the modern world and the United States gained a firm hold in Hawaii.

Plantation owners turned profits back into machinery. In 1915 Grove Farm bought two Model-T Ford trucks for light hauling and two caterpillar tractors to pull the plows. In the 1920's, a mechanical cane planter was developed. Now sugar was undisputed king of Hawaii and the wealthy planters became as powerful as the old Hawaiian chiefs had once been. A few of the old plantation mansions still stand proudly behind their tree-lined drives, reflecting their period of power.

In contrast to the sybaritic lives of the plantation masters, living conditions of the workers were harsh. Managers ruled like despots and a few acquired a reputation for pure cruelty. At Koloa, a Prussian named W.E. Anton Cropp kept a small dungeon

MISSIONARY GRANDDAUGHTER, Miss Mabel Wilcox, sits in her Grove Farm home amidst family memorabilia. Her grandparents came to Hanalei in 1846, bringing Protestantism to the area.

where he imprisoned balky workers. Resistance to the inequities began to appear. From 1902 on, strikes broke out on one plantation or another. The labor unrest came to a climax in 1946. Every mill, plantation, and irrigation ditch was shut down. When this destructive strike was settled, a better balance of power was established between labor and management. Today sugar workers on Kauai are among the highest paid in the world.

Kauai has a life style all its own. The language is English spiced with pidgin. Fast food hamburger stands and shops that sell noodles operate against the jagged mountain skyline. Pretty girls in bikinis stroll the beaches where Hawaiian fishermen throw their nets. Boutiques have sprung up in the plantation camps among sugar cane fields. Tour buses park in rows in front of air conditioned hotels.

The pattern for all this was set in 1898 when Hawaii became a U.S. Territory. This gave the residents of Kauai U.S. citizenship and a new national holiday, the 4th of July.

Faces on the island were steadily changing in both numbers and complexion. The decreasing population hit a low of 5,000 in 1872 but gradually recovered to over 20,000 by 1920. The recovery was due to sugar.

Planting and harvesting cane, weeding, tending the irrigation ditches, all required a large labor force. This sparsely populated island could not supply it, so workers were imported —first from China, then Japan, later from Europe, Korea and the island of Madeira. The workers were housed in plantation camps scattered all over the island, and of course brought with them customs and habits that help to make up the exciting, picturesque complex that Kauai is today. Hanapepe, Kalaheo, Puhi, Hanamaulu, Kapaa, Kealia are Kauai villages that evolved from past plantation camps.

Statehood for Hawaii came in 1959. With statehood came many changes. Great numbers of tourists are now landing at Lihue Airport in the midst of a sugar cane field. Poipu Beach, just down from Koloa landing

TASSELED SUGAR CANE frames Mount Waialeale. Kauai's fields have produced world-record sugar crops—as high as 18 tons an acre. Above, retired 70-year-old cook, Sonny Leong, tells of the early days.

IN A TIMELESS MOMENT OF BEAUTY, a fisherman casts his net. Peaceful Hanapepe Town is reflected in the serene surface of its river flowing gently to join the waters of Port Allen.

where whalers had once anchored, became a resort center. Hotels sprang up between Wailua and Kapaa where only coconut palms had stood before.

Some of the tourists wore their hair long and carried packs on their backs. Most of these visitors returned home after their island adventure. Others remained on the island, finding jobs in the new hotels and restaurants. They constitute a new immigrant labor force. Their bosses are often descendants of Oriental plantation workers. Many of the customers they serve are tourists from Japan who now make up a substantial number of visitors here.

The population of Kauai County is now about 34,000 and still growing. The island is linked to the outside world by telephone, radio, satellite and daily flights by air from Honolulu. Many of the old plantation camps have been replaced by modern subdivisions. The economic symbols on Kauai today are giant cane haul trucks and air conditioned tour buses.

Yet, Kauai remains the most remote and least changed of all the major islands in Hawaii. Countless tons of rain still fall daily on Mount Waialeale, and Alakai Swamp is still as eerie a place as you can find on earth. Jagged mountain peaks still rise against the sky, proof that this special island was sculptured by the gods.

Kauai Today

I t's fun to capture the off-beat flavor of Kauai. Each day is a modern experience in an ancient setting. It's a crazy combination of tropical wonderland and everyday living. Kauai is a South Sea sunrise over an air conditioned super market against a backdrop of volcanic mountains. The girl waiting on your table for breakfast may go surfing in the afternoon. Or exercise her horse along the beach in preparation for the Aloha Week parade. The glass and chrome library in sunny Koloa is where the archaeology club meets to plan excavations of ancient ruins. On Kauai, outrigger canoe racing is as important to people as Sunday morning professional football on television. The way to enjoy all this is to slow down and let it sink in.

An advantage for visitors to Kauai is its small size. Its wonders of nature, 1,500 years of history and half a dozen cultures are packed into an island only 33 miles long and 25 miles wide. Forests of tasseled sugar cane open without warning on sun-drenched villages and picturesque churches. Placid Buddhas pop up in Oriental cemeteries every few miles along the road. The distance between busy Lihue Airport and sleepy Waimea Bay where Captain Cook first landed can be covered in less than an hour by car. But the two places are 200 miles apart in atmosphere. All this means that it's foolish to hurry on Kauai. The faster you go, the more you will miss along the way. On this microcosm of a Pacific island, the smiles you collect are more important than the miles you cover.

INTO WIND-DRIVEN SPRAY (below) canoeists surge from shore at the start of the "Iron Man" race, 12 miles of hard paddling from Kauai's Wailua River to Nawiliwili Bay. At far left, two young fishermen hold up handsome sailfish. In center, a Hobie Cat darts across waters of Nawiliwili Bay, while a beautiful young girl exercises her horse along a beach.

HORSE AND PA'U RIDER are draped in leis of Kauai colors for annual Oahu Kamehameha Day festivities. Below, Jack Harter deposits visitors on Kauai's Napali Coast for a day's outing. Harter and his wife, Beverly, run Garden Island Helicopters, carrying visitors everywhere on the island from their Heliport near the Kauai Surf Hotel.

BRIGHT IN THE MORNING SUN, sugar cane (above) surrounds new community college at Puhi . . . a pretty Eurasian girl works as a stewardess for Hawaiian Airlines . . . and a Kauai cemetery shows the many racial groups which have melded to make today's polyracial island society.

ENCHANTED HIKER PAUSES ON THE TRAIL to Kalalau. Above, Dr. Bernard Wheatley walks the Napali beach outside his cave home.

The Valley of Refuge

On the Napali Coast of Kauai where canyons guarded by 3,000-foot cliffs have resisted the inroads of civilization, is the hidden Valley of Kalalau. On this remote shore, the place that most titillates the imagination, Kalalau Valley, remains shrouded in mystery and legend, inaccessible to all but the most adventurous, a refuge from oppression for people of free spirit.

It has always been so. The first Hawaiian settlers found a tropical paradise, a fertile valley four miles deep, adorned with waterfalls, protected by soaring cliffs. Here the first people grew to a numerous clan. They industriously terraced every arable foot of land for taro production. For more than 1,000 years they worshipped their gods, en-

joyed the zest of youth, begat children, grew to old age and rejoined their ancestors. They did all this without fear of invasion because the mountain passes were easily defended and the only other entry was by the turbulent sea.

Such isolation lost much of its appeal after the white man established new and exciting centers of population. Like country people everywhere, the residents of Kalalau Valley gradually moved away to town. By 1892 only a few inhabitants still worked their taro patches.

Kalalau Valley gradually slipped into somnolent isolation broken only by wild pig hunters or fishermen. The years went by. Then, one day in the mid-1950's, a black man, a medical doctor from the Virgin Islands, stood at Kokee lookout and gazed down into the vast, green sanctuary of the valley. The man's name was Bernard Wheatley. He had experienced a religious conversion, given away all of his earthly possessions, turned his back on medicine, and was searching for eternal truth.

K alalau Valley was the haven long sought. Although not equipped for camping, carrying only a lunch, he followed the trail that winds high along Napali. After a hard 10 miles of hiking he reached the haven of Kalalau Valley. There he found shelter in a cave beneath a towering black cliff overlooking the beach. Wheatley stayed in the valley for 23 days, until he became ill and was carried by a passing fishing sampan to Lihue for hospital care.

Five weeks later he was back in the valley, but this time armed with a mess kit and a change of clothing. He lived off guavas, taro, mangoes, bananas, oranges and papayas. Hunters and campers gave extra food to Wheatley when they left. But he seldom accepted invitations to eat with them.

"Most people think I am crazy," he said matter-of-factly to a visitor. "They can't wait to tell me what a big fool I am because I don't work, have abandoned a medical practice, and am not interested in the approval of society. However, when they realize I am quite intelligent and well educated, people who are not very well educated tend to become frightened of me. Also, if I accept an invitation to eat with them, they invariably feel this gives them the right to force their opinions on me. I have a violent temper, and I prefer to avoid such provocations."

Wheatley put his visitors up in a guest cave near his own. He asked them not to walk indiscriminately across the great, tawny beach in front of the caves. "Do you see those geometrical patterns?" he would say. "These are my paths. May I ask you to use them? There is great beauty in the sand when the sun or moonlight outlines the ripples made by the wind. Footprints destroy the perfection of the ripples. I have found that, of all the requirements for survival, beauty is the most important."

His cave was arranged with the Spartan austerity of a monk's cell. The sand floor was carefully swept. Silverware and cooking utensils were in a niche in the wall. "I always set my table (a wooden box) correctly with silverware at meals," he said, "even though I am having only taro. One can judge character

by the way a man acts in the wilderness."

Wheatley showered beneath a waterfall near his cave. He learned to chase and catch mountain goats on the cliffs for meat. He knocked mangoes out of trees by throwing rocks. Yet, his main concern was to find the truth. "The problem is that most people do not act out what they say they believe," he said. "There are many obvious examples. We say, 'Thou shalt not kill.' Yet during wartime we give medals for killing. We say, 'Thou shalt not covet.' Yet our whole economy is built on the desire to own things. The last paying position I held was that of clerk at the YMCA. I quit because I was told to charge a man who couldn't pay for a room.

"I know I am considered an idler. Gandhi was, after all, an educated idler. Here in Kalalau Valley I feel very close to God. My relationship to Him must be similar to that of Abraham's. There is more here than just quietness. There is a big peace. There is music in the wind and the surf. I like sundown best and the moonlight on the ripples in the sand. I like to sit in my cave and watch Venus in the night sky."

Wheatley, the hermit of Kalalau, remained in the valley for several years before he gave the outside world another try. The reentry experience was not as satisfying as he had hoped, so he went back to Kalalau. However, by now other seekers of solitude were also finding their way over the Napali trail. Few of these young vagabonds had Wheatley's education, intelligence or discipline. Wheatley is no longer there.

Instead, he has become a legend, a folk hero to the steady stream of hikers who turn their faces to the mist-shrouded cliffs of the Napali Coast hoping to solve the mystery of themselves in Kalalau Valley.

SOLITARY HIKER along cliff trail to Kalalau Valley.

The Island of Kauai

KAUAI IS THE FOURTH LARGEST ISLAND in the Hawaiian chain. It is 553.3 square miles or 352,640 acres in size, 110 miles in circumference, and is located 103 air miles from Honolulu's airport on Oahu. Access by sea is across the Kauai Channel. Kauai's dormant volcano, Kawaikini, is the eighth highest peak in the state at 5,243 feet above sea level.

POPULATION OF KAUAI is approximately 34,000 with a population density of 53.8 per square mile. Lihue is the county seat, and Kauai's largest town.

ETHNIC MAKEUP is 9% Hawaiian, 26% Caucasian, 2% Chinese, 33% Japanese, 28% Filipino, and 2% other.

CLIMATE AND TEMPERATURE. Like Oahu and the other major islands in the Hawaiian chain, Kauai enjoys a place in the middle of a sunny ocean, with cooling trade winds most of the year, and ample rainfall. The warmest months are August and September, the coolest are January and February. Average temperatures at Lihue range from 70° in the coolest month, to 78° in the warmest.

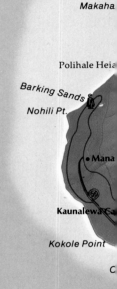

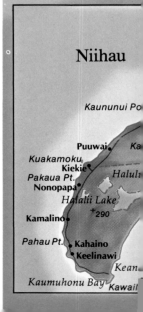

KAUAI

STATUTE MILES

0   2   4   6   8

STATUTE MILES

2   4   6

CASCADES OF GREEN (at right) crown the Fern Grotto.

Lihue to Haena

Lihue—The total population of this over-grown plantation camp, about 7,000, would fit into the bleachers of any major league ballpark. Yet, Lihue is full of surprises for a curious visitor. There's an operating sugar mill in the middle of everything (above). Not far away an old world Lutheran church (below) looks as incongruous amidst tropical foliage as a tiny Japanese cemetery down the hill. As the county seat, Lihue is the place to pick up camping permits. Banks are located here, and Wilcox Memorial Hospital. Also a modern shopping center that grew out of the plantation store.

Wailua Falls—About a mile from Lihue past the airport road, a sign in a hollow shows you where to turn to Wailua Falls. It's four miles farther on. The falls thunder over a 50-foot cliff into a misty pool in a setting of hala trees. Young Hawaiians used to impress their girl friends by jumping over the falls.

Hanamaulu—This village began as a plantation camp in 1875. The fields were so far from Lihue mill, 3 miles, that it was easier to build a mill here than to take harvested sugar cane three miles by ox cart to Lihue. Hanamaulu mill was abandoned in 1918 but the village remains as a picturesque reminder of Kauai's past.

Wailua Golf Course—Everyone is welcome to play here. The course is maintained by the county. You'll pass the clubhouse on the right side of the highway.

Wailua River—Now you've come to one of the special places on Kauai. Wailua means "sacred" or "ghostly water." Here the chiefs of Kauai, bluest-blooded of Hawaii's pagan aristocrats, conducted their most important ceremonies. Source of the stream (above) is Mount Waialeale, abode of the gods, in the center of the island (page 10).

Fern Grotto—On the near side of the river, a short drive on the left leads to a landing where boats take passengers upstream to a

hoary old lava tube buried in the jungle. This is the Fern Grotto, a scene that inspires romance. Many weddings take place in this cave festooned with ferns. The minimum fee, including minister, is $100.

Lydgate Park—On the other side of the highway is a public park good for picnicking, camping (by permit) or swimming. Here also are the ruins of old Hawaiian stone walls that once enclosed a temple. It is the last in a string of seven heiaus that begin at the top of Mount Waialeale.

Ancient Trail—The first road inland after crossing the river follows an ancient trail along the string of temples. Just beyond the coconut grove is one of them; Holo-Holo-Ku, a sacred refuge where victims of the kapus could escape to safety. The name means "to run (and) stand (in safety)." Hawaiian chiefesses gave birth on stones nearby. The road continues uphill to an overlook with a spectacular view of Wailua River and rice paddies. Farther on, a turnoff leads to the Bell Stone, a rock that gives off a "bong" when struck. It was used to announce the approach of chiefs and chiefesses. Another heiau, Poliahu, stands at the top of the hill. The enclosure contains phallic images. One of Kauai's loveliest waterfalls, Opaikaa, is farther on, silver threads drifting down over a black lava cliff.

Sleeping Giant—Resort hotels have sprung up along the shore beyond Wailua. A little less than two miles from the river, glance at the mountain skyline. You'll see a giant, sleeping on his back. He's been there since Menehunes tried to waken him by throwing rocks. Quite a number landed in his mouth. He swallowed them in his sleep, developed a severe case of indigestion and never woke up.

Kapaa Town—Here's an opportunity to catch a glimpse of plantation days. Some of the old stores have been repaired and have begun new careers selling souvenirs and sport clothes.

St. Catherine's Catholic Church—This is one of those delightful surprises Kauai is full of. Two miles from Kapaa turn uphill. On the plateau is a country church full of art work by Juliette May Fraser, Tseng Yu Ho and Jean Charlot. They are all friends of the unusual priest who built the church.

Kealia—This is the shanty town remains of a plantation camp. It's at the other end of the beach from the church.

Waipahee Slide—Waipahee means "slippery water." It refers to a natural slippery

slide in a stream inland from Kealia. Swimmers can shoot along an eroded lava tube and out over a pool 18 feet deep. It's not easy to find. Take the Kealia Road at the rodeo corral in the village 2-1/2 miles to Spaulding Monument in the cane fields. Turn left and go another 2-1/2 miles to the end of the road. Then take the trail to the slide. If it's muddy, forget it.

Anahola—About six miles from Kealia you'll come to a sign across from a school that points to Anahola Beach. The road dips down into a sunny valley to a magnificent beach that curves in a tremendous arc around the bay. This is a marvelous place to swim and picnic. Camping by permit. Anahola is a Hawaiian settlement discovered by lots of other people.

Moloaa Beach—There's another turnoff ahead to a sunlit, secluded beach whose name means "matted roots." The valley behind the beach is a tangle of hau trees.

Blue-Faced Boobies—The next village is Kilauea. Turn right in the center of town to the lighthouse (above) on a cliff overlooking the Pacific. This is a nesting place for blue-faced boobies whose comic antics and graceful flight provide lots of free entertainment.

Anini Beach—Now you are approaching one of the most beautiful places in the world. You will cross behind breathtaking Kalihiwai Beach. The next one is Anini. A side road hiccups past meadows and cottages and lovely beaches before it gets lost in the jungle. Here you'll find a picnic pavilion.

Princeville—The high plateau beyond was once a plantation. Now it's being turned into

a fabulous resort that some people have called "Paradise Improved." The complex features three Robert Trent Jones, Jr., golf courses plus tennis courts everywhere.

Hanalei—From here you must not hurry. A bend ahead offers a magnificent view of Hanalei Valley (above). Then the road descends to the village tucked amid tropical foliage behind the bay. This place is worth exploring. There's an old mission house, the majestic beach, country stores, and another Catholic church containing art work.

Lumahai Beach—Lumahai, one of the most photographed places on Kauai, is two miles from Hanalei. You can get to the sand on a path from the turnout above the beach.

Wainiha Valley—Now you are in Menehune country because Wainiha Valley was their favorite residence (page 31). On the far side a road leads into deep jungle back into the valley where electrical power is generated from waterfalls.

Haena—Beyond Wainiha Valley lies a world of magic alive with ghosts and dreams and romance (page 26). The jagged mountains and vivid blossoms and angular hala trees (page 23) are just as Gaugin would have painted them.

The Caves—The first cave just ahead, according to legend, was dug by Menehunes. The next two were dug by Pele, goddess of volcanoes (page 26). All three are marked by signs and are easy to find on foot.

Napali Coast—The road ends at a delightful beach where you can see the Napali Coast looming ahead. Here also is the beginning of the nine-mile foot trail that leads to Kalalau Valley (page 55). There's an ancient hula temple on the black lava point beyond the beach.

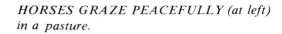

HORSES GRAZE PEACEFULLY (at left) in a pasture.

Lihue to Waimea

Nawiliwili—This is the principal port on Kauai where you can watch sugar being loaded on ships. To get there, drive past the County Building and follow your nose until

you reach the sea. The harbor is in a picturesque hollow and is fringed by a beautiful sand beach (above). Follow a road back through the tropical foliage instead of going back the way you came.

65

Alekoko Fish Pond—One reason is because this is the way to the famous Menehune Fish Pond (page 31). Besides, the drive is delightful. From the fish pond, you can circle back to Lihue or continue on around the island.

Grove Farm Homestead—The highway leading out of Lihue going in the opposite direction from Nawiliwili will take you down into a hollow and past the mill. Circle left on the next turnoff. Tucked behind that curve is an interesting cemetery where many of the people are buried who made Kauai's history. Farther on is the old Grove Farm plantation house which is being turned into a museum. It's not ready for viewing.

Koloa—Now go back to the highway and continue on. You'll pass the Kauai Community College Campus on the right and the old Puhi Plantation Store on the left. Seven miles from Lihue there's a turnoff to the left leading through a tunnel of trees. Beyond is the village of Koloa; the old mill, quaint stores, a Buddhist temple and plenty of sunshine.

beach park (above). There are more beaches for hikers beyond the lighthouse.

Poipu Shore—It's only a few miles from Koloa to the sea where hotels have sprung up along some of the most beautiful beaches on Kauai. Here there's surfing and a public

Spouting Horn—Tour buses are constantly lined up here to permit passengers to view the geyser spouting from an underwater lava tube (page 29). On the way you will pass a grassy little park which marks where Prince Kuhio was born. He was a cousin of King Kalakaua and Queen Liliuokalani and a long time delegate to Congress from Hawaii.

Eighty-eight Holy Places—From Koloa you have a choice between two routes around the island. Go back to the highway the way you came or turn left out of Koloa and wander through a gorgeous rolling countryside framed in mountains for about four miles. You'll come out again on the highway. Just 2/10 of a mile beyond there's an opening on the Koloa side of the highway. It leads to an interesting hillside shrine called the 88 Holy Places, one for each sin committed by man. Pilgrims come here to be released from these sins.

Kukuiolono Park—The next village is Kalahoe, a picturesque and prosperous Portuguese settlement. A road leading uphill will take you to the former estate of sugar magnate Walter McBryde who donated it for a park. The high, sloping plateau has been turned into a golf course. The views are magnificent. There's also a tropical garden. In ancient times this high ground was where signal fires showed Hawaiian fishermen the way home from far at sea.

Hanapepe Valley—Stop at the next viewpoint on the highway. This is where most people reach for their cameras to snap the mottled greens and burnt earth colors of Hanapepe Valley.

Hanapepe Town—A sweeping curve brings you down into a hollow. Take a turnoff to the right into one of the most charming country towns in Hawaii (page 47). The name means literally "crushed bay," the result of landslides. Today, false-fronted stores and balconies face a wide, curving street.

Salt Ponds—Just beyond Hanapepe, a turnoff to the left takes you through a dreary, bare plain that is flooded with sea water to make salt by evaporation. There's a dandy swimming beach at the end of the road, and a view of Port Allen, Kauai's second harbor.

Russian Fort—The next town is Waimea. Before you enter the village, there's a stairway with an iron railing that leads up into the trees. This is the short trail to the historic old Russian Fort (page 41).

Waimea—Wooden frame construction has replaced the grass thatch that Captain James Cook saw here in 1778. Yet, Waimea remains one of the most picturesque places on Kauai. There's the old mission church on the hill, turn-of-the-century stores and a view of the bay where white men first landed.

Menehune Ditch—A road beneath the bluff leads back into the valley where Hawaiians once irrigated taro. Now it's returned to weeds and forest. The old trail is a narrow road running past dilapidated houses. Turn toward the cliffs 6/10 of a mile from the highway to see a charming temple with 88 more shrines. The Menehune Ditch is 2-1/2 miles from the highway under an old, suspension footbridge.

Kekaha—This plantation town, complete with mill, is the jumping off place for Waimea Canyon. But you can continue on a little farther around the island if you like.

Mana—That island offshore is Niihau. Eight miles beyond Kekaha is the hamlet of Mana and, farther on, the road ends at Polihale State Park & Heiau. It's a lonely, sun drenched spot. The Napali Cliffs loom in the distance.

Waimea Canyon—From Kekaha the Waimea Canyon road winds up and up into bracing air and soaring vistas. The vegetation changes from lowland haole koa and cactus to upland silver oak and native koa. There are numerous lookouts over the canyon including the one way at the top over Kalalau Valley (above). Foot trails maintained by rangers lead through the forest. Near the top you'll find a lodge and museum.

The Resorts

Kauai's resort hotels are clustered in four general areas. All the areas are equipped with good restaurants and beaches. Distances are not so great on Kauai that you can't explore the whole island from any of the resort clusters. We've defined luxury hotels as those which charge over $40 per double room, superior hotels as those which charge roughly $30 to $40 and deluxe hotels as those which charge under $30. A few places charge under $20. You can make your own reservations or have it done free of charge by any travel agent.

Wailua-Kapaa

This cluster of resorts is located seven to ten miles from the airport in Lihue. The hotels are strung along a coastline of beaches and palm trees. There's a golf course in the area.

Coco Palms Resort—Low rise accommo-dations on a lagoon in a coconut grove. Nightly entertainment, romantic surroundings and imaginative decor (such as clam shell wash basins). Luxury.

Kapaa Sands Hotel—Duplex houses on a small beach. Pool but no dining room or bar. Luxury.

Holiday Inn Kauai Beach—A quality, beachfront resort hotel located in the 103-acre Coconut Plantation resort at Waipouli, approximately six miles north of Lihue. The hotel contains 311 guest rooms each with lanai, wall-to-wall carpeting, color television and central air conditioning. Nearly 80% of the rooms have ocean views. The hotel lobby features a four-story waterfall and reflect-ing pools. Also included are a dining room, cocktail lounge, show room, meeting room, poolside snack bar and retail shops. Other amenities include a swimming pool, sun deck, putting green, tennis courts and extensive landscaped grounds. Superior.

Islander Inn—Located in the Coconut Plantation resort and shopping complex. Beach and pool. Superior.

Kauai Beach Boy—Also in the Coconut Plantation. Pool, shops, bar, dance floor. Superior.

Kauai Sands—Locally owned, friendly staff. Deluxe.

Kauai Resort Hotel—Near Lydgate Park, pool, access to park beach. Superior to deluxe.

Hotel Coral Reef—In Kapaa, small beach, palm trees, below $20.

Poipu

The weather at Poipu is much like that in Waikiki, mostly sunny. This is an area of lovely beaches, safe swimming and good surfing. Poipu doesn't have an 18-hole golf course, only 9 holes for pitch and putt. There are tennis courts. It's ten miles from the airport.

Sheraton-Kauai Hotel—Well appointed, big hotel, dramatic dining room, shops, entertainment. Right on the beach. Luxury.

Waiohai Hotel—Intimate, informal atmosphere. There's a pitch and putt golf course, low rise buildings, beautiful beach. Luxury.

Kiohuna Beach Houses—Thirty-one cottages with 200 units, tennis courts, pool. Luxury.

Poipu Beach Hotel—Open air lobby, pool, lovely beach. Superior.

Hale Nani of Kauai—A-frame cottages located at Koloa Landing, pool. Superior.

Nawiliwili-Lihue

This cluster of hotels is located only a mile or two from the airport. From here it's about the same distance either way to the ends of the road around the island. The deluxe hotels in Lihue are several miles from a beach.

Kauai Surf Hotel—This is the only "skyscraper" (11 stories) on the island. It's set behind a gorgeous beach, is equipped with tennis courts and an 18-hole golf course. Pool, restaurants, entertainment. Luxury.

I Pali Kai Cottages—Condos located near the Kauai Surf and the golf course. Luxury.

Ocean View Motel—Patronized by backpackers and bikers, no frills, under $20.

Tip Top Motel—A venerable institution in Lihue. Salesmen, construction workers stay here. Under $20.

70

Hanalei

This is the most remote cluster of resorts on the island, about 40 miles from the airport. The area boasts one of the two best golf courses in the state. The beaches are superb and the peaceful atmosphere is all pervasive.

Hanalei Colony Resort—Small, informal, comfortable hotel almost at the end of the road, nice beach, restaurant. Superior.

Princeville Makai Golf Cottages—This is part of a recreational community now being developed. Condo units are convenient to golf course, tennis courts and pool. Not on the beach. Luxury.

Club Mediterranee—Secluded, great view over Hanalei Bay, pool, restaurant, beach. Luxury.

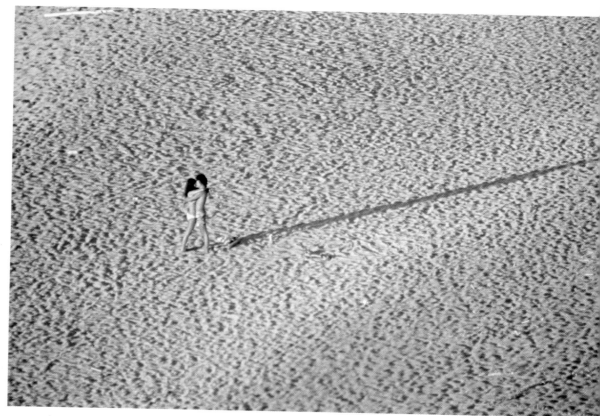

Hawaiian Airlines is proud to have helped in the creation of this remarkable book about Kauai. In 1979 Hawaiian marks its 50th anniversary, carrying over three million passengers annually. Hawaiian Airlines inaugurated scheduled service between the islands on November 11, 1929—a time when even an automobile trip was an adventure. Hawaiian continues to serve all who reside in the 50th state and the millions of visitors who come each year to share Hawaii's natural beauty. The friendly people of Hawaiian Air will help you see all of Hawaiian's islands.

PHOTO CREDITS

Cover, Bill Gleasner; p. 1, Bill Gleasner; pp. 2-3, Bill Gleasner; pp. 4-5, Iooss from Starr/McCombs, Inc.; pp. 6-7, Bill Gleasner; pp. 8-9, Bill Gleasner; pp. 10-11, Bill Gleasner; pp. 12-13, Bill Gleasner; pp. 14-15, Bill Gleasner; pp. 16-17, Bill Gleasner; p. 18, Bill Gleasner; p. 19, *Illustrated Atlas of Hawaii*; p. 20, Herb Kane; p. 21, left, Robert B. Goodman; right, Bill Gleasner; p. 22, *Illustrated Atlas of Hawaii*; p. 23, Bill Gleasner; pp. 24-25, Bill Gleasner; pp. 26-27, Iooss from Starr/McCombs, Inc.; p. 28, Iooss from Starr/McCombs, Inc.; p. 29, Bill Gleasner; pp. 30-31, Bill Gleasner; pp. 32-33, Bill Gleasner; pp. 34-35, Herb Kane from *Voyage*; pp. 36-37, Herb Kane from *Voyage*; p. 38, Herb Kane; p. 39, from the collection of Terence Barrow; p. 40, painting by Joseph Feher; p. 41, from the collection of Don Severson; pp. 42-43, Robert B. Goodman; pp. 44-45, Bill Gleasner; pp. 46-47, Bill Gleasner; pp. 48-49, Bill Gleasner; pp. 50-51, Bill Gleasner; pp. 52-53, Bill Gleasner and Hawaiian Airlines; p. 54, Bill Gleasner; p. 55, Robert B. Goodman; p. 57, Bill Gleasner; p. 60, Bill Gleasner and Hawaiian Airlines; p. 61, Hawaiian Airlines; p. 62, Iooss from Starr/McCombs, Inc.; p. 63, Bill Gleasner and Bud Thuener; p. 64, Bill Gleasner; center, Iooss from Starr/McCombs, Inc.; p. 65, top, Bill Gleasner; bottom, Bud Thuener; pp. 66-67, Bill Gleasner; p. 68, Morton Beebe; p. 69, Iooss from Starr/McCombs, Inc.; p. 70, Iooss from Starr/McCombs, Inc.; p. 71, top, Doug Jones from Fawcett McDermott Cavanagh, Inc.; bottom, Bill Gleasner.